Lucky Life Lessons

A Guide to Cultivating Luck and Positive Energy in Your Life

TONY WARGO

Copyright © 2012 Tony Wargo

All rights reserved.

ISBN: 0615647901
ISBN-13: 9780615647906

DEDICATION

This book is dedicated to my daughter, Olivia Noelle, for making me the luckiest man alive.

CONTENTS

Acknowledgments

Introduction

Part I

1	What Is Luck?	Pg. 1
2	Luck Can't Be Manipulated or Controlled	Pg. 7
3	The Lucky Penny Rule	Pg. 11

Part II

4	Recognize It In Every Form	Pg. 19
5	Show Appreciation	Pg. 23
6	Learn to Recognize Its Presence	Pg. 29
7	Treat It As A Friendly Being	Pg. 35
8	Not Spoken Of	Pg. 39
9	Never Take It For Granted	Pg. 47
	Conclusion	Pg. 51

ACKNOWLEDGMENTS

While this book focuses on luck and positive energy, I give all the glory and honor to the Lord. His daily blessings are the true source of my luck and good fortune. My Catholic faith, the Church community of Immaculate Conception in Hampton ,VA and all the mystery that surrounds us have blessed my life. Thank you to Daryl Cash and Stacey Salerno for always offering to help with my design needs. Thanks to Zack Bevelacqua for the science experiment information. Lastly, I want to thank my wife for her endless patience, help and support in writing this book as well as everything I do.

I love you Jen.

INTRODUCTION

This book is real. You are holding it and you can see it. There is no denying its existence. The ideas and thoughts contained within are real as well. You can see them as words on the pages and by holding this book, you are holding them as well. I leave it up to the reader to determine the reality of what is true. I have always been blessed with luck and surrounded by positive energy.

To write this book is to speak of a natural part of my life. What many will read and put into practice is a natural occurrence and standard of living in my world. While certain influences bind me from revealing all the sources of what I am about to share, I have been guided to release some aspects that the common reader will find plentiful and useful. The most I will share about my source is that when I was three years old, I had a very profound, uncommon, not of this world experience that has and always will remain a secret. It was a very positive and magical moment that brought me to a point of no return, so to speak. It is impossible to "un-know" or "un-see" something once it has occurred.

Some reading this book will consider it to be fiction and for entertainment only. For those who believe that, they will be accurate in their opinion. You will learn more about what I mean as you read and understand what follows.

For those who approach this book with an open mind and understanding of the possibilities of the potential this book holds, you will set your limits and boundaries of how much luck and positive energy you allow to enter into your life. Please don't just take these words as truth. As a friendly challenge, I encourage you to treat this book as a guide and handbook and watch the incredible transformation your life will encounter. Good luck!

How to use this book- I have decided it is best to split this book into two parts. The first part is mostly informational. I may include some tips or instructions along the way, but it is my intention to use the first part to inform the reader. The second part of the book can be considered the "how-to" guide or instruction manual for luck and positive energy.

I'm sure there are going to be some that are going to want to jump right to part two and skip part one. Many items come with instruction manuals that people toss aside because they want to immediately begin playing with their new gadget, toy or device. That may work with common items or man-made machinery, but what this book is addressing isn't something that you can just pick up and start using.

It is extremely important to develop an understanding of luck and positive energy before you apply the concepts introduced in part II. Everything I describe has been a natural part of my life, just like breathing. The challenges I faced with writing this book are ways to capture the intangible and accurately define and describe with words something that is indescribable.

The best way I can think to illustrate my challenge is to ask the reader to describe the beauty of color and the location of the beginning source and ending point of natural wind. I did my best to explain everything in the simplest form possible so to be comprehended and understood by all.

You will notice as you read that I speak of luck and positive energy as if they are living and breathing beings. I consider them to be so and have experienced them in that manner. I know of no other way to refer to them. I have one last thought related to value I'd like to mention before getting started. This book is probably not the largest book you've read in your lifetime. Truly I tell you that I struggled with the length of this book. I reviewed it dozens of times and ultimately determined it's where it needs to be. I could very easily have padded it with boring and useless narratives to make it a lot longer. However, the information contained within is truly priceless, extremely useful and very powerful. An extreme amount of knowledge and power can be contained in a very small amount of information. To illustrate this point, one simply has to look at the summation of Albert Einstein's theory of relativity in what is probably one of the best known equations. $E=MC^2$.

PART I

1 WHAT IS LUCK?

Is luck something that is real? For some it is. Others may call it chance. For those that believe in luck, they may think some have more than others. I hear about luck all the time. I even hear people say the words "bad luck" together. I find great humor in that mindset. Luck can never be bad! For some unknown reason, this thought has been accepted by a large amount of people. Replace the word "luck" with other words that denote something good and you will hear from my perspective how absurd it sounds. Some examples are bad love, bad bliss, bad peace, and bad happiness. Hopefully you get the point. I'm sure there are plenty of other examples that can be used and feel free to have fun with it if it helps you understand that luck, by its very nature, cannot be bad. I am here to defend luck and all it stands for!

Some may ask if it is even real. Of course it's real! Not everyone is as open to the reality of its existence, but that doesn't negate it. Some people deny the existence of true love, but there are plenty of people to testify to the reality and power of love. It is an endless source that has no boundaries and like all matter, it cannot be created nor destroyed. How often have you heard people acknowledge luck in their life or someone else's life? Have you ever heard of a spectacular event occurring and some or many say that luck was involved? I love hearing about people who are on a winning streak or a lucky streak. They are experiencing the force of luck and doing some of the things I will share with you, possibly without even realizing it. I love the first definition of luck according to the Merriam-

Webster Dictionary- "a force that brings good fortune or adversity." It is literally defined as a force! Luck is different than superstition. If you do research you will find that just about every superstition that is commonly accepted has its roots in a historically documented event.

There may be some people saying that it is chance. Others may say that luck is proven through probabilities or statistics. My response to that is that science is always trying to find a way to prove nature for all the wonderful beauties it provides. Rather than accepting and enjoying what nature and life has to offer, humans feel the need to set parameters and decode with a provable and rational system. This book is going to provide an understanding of the beauty of luck so that it can be accepted and enjoyed rather than proven and measured. If you don't accept that it is real or at least accept the possibility that it is real, there is nothing I can do to change your mind. I still encourage you to read further and listen to my words.

I've also heard people say that some people have more luck than others. They will somehow trace it back to a root cause like a talent, special ability or even high intelligence to provide reasoning as to why things work out the way they do. These may be legit reasons, but I'm willing to bet that if you look closely, you'll see where luck has inserted itself somewhere.

Luck is humble and soft-spoken. It wants to be known, but not the center of attention. Picture a flame on a candle. It is a simple reaction resulting from a match or a lighter creating a flame and transferring it to the wick. The oxygen in the room provides the medium for the flame to continue to exist. If left alone, the flame will continue to burn very slowly and remain still. If there is a change in the direction of air, it will cause the flame to move about delicately in a dancing motion, but will not be extinguished. If the conditions are right and flammable materials are introduced to the flame, the small flame will grow and spread. The properties of it will not change. It is still fire only there will be more of it until there is no longer the proper conditions for it to exist. In a sense, I want you to think of luck as an eternal flame burning and your life is combustible. There will be plenty more on this later, but for now keep that filed away in the back of your mind.

2 LUCK CAN'T BE MANIPULATED OR CONTROLLED

I have discovered that ultimately, luck decides when to play and when to not play. I can do my best to try and describe the rules and guidelines to follow to maximize your chances of increasing luck and positive energy in your life, but it is a natural force that determines the boundaries in which it exists. Luck has always been around and is an ancient source of energy. It is infinite in its reach and source. It is also wise and clever enough to know when to get involved. There have been numerous times when I've hoped luck will play a role and that's about all I can do- hope! I still haven't figured out what dictates when luck will occur other than you just have to be lucky.

Something that you might feel compelled to do is to get angry or negative when you aren't lucky or lose or someone else is lucky. Never blame it for not "working". Use extreme forgiveness and patience as you would with a child. Life is supposed to be fun and you can't win all the time or be the only lucky person in town. If you lose to someone else be happy for them and the positive feelings they are experiencing. Everyone is just as deserving of a good time as the next person.

Trust me when I say there is plenty of good luck and positive energy for every single person in the world thousands of times over. You will soon discover that once a relationship is established, communication and understanding is developed. That may not make much sense now, but the smiles will appear on your face more frequently and you'll find yourself letting go and laughing a lot more often than before you started reading this book.

Take this moment right now as you read that last sentence and this one. Did you smile a little or at least picture yourself smiling more? Did you doubt the idea of smiling more just because you read something in a book? If you smiled or even thought about it, I encourage you to take a moment right now and enjoy a couple deep breaths and soak up those smiles and positive feelings. If you had doubts, don't be discouraged! Your luck has already changed.   Just by realizing that just as much luck belongs to you as the one considered being the luckiest person alive should put a smile on your face. Reading this book alone will increase your focus on luck and positive energy enough to bring them into your life without any effort on your part. Simply being aware and acknowledging that it is a part of life and a natural force is all you need. So if you haven't smiled by now, I see a big smile in your near future.

Much the same as with people, luck is very loyal and there when you truly need it. It has always been a very loyal friend of mine.

3 THE LUCKY PENNY RULE

I decided to include this chapter to share an example of a simple change you can begin to make that will potentially double the amount of free money you obtain by luck. I was in deep thought one day as I often am, and had an epiphany. I mentioned superstition at one point earlier, but never really went into detail about. After all this talk about luck I would like to declare that I am in no way superstitious.

Superstitions are absurd and have no validity or proof. They are merely based on gossip and fueled by people's fears. In the past, when I would see a penny on the ground, I wouldn't view it as lucky if it was on tails. The common thought is that it's "bad luck" (there's that phrase again) if a penny is on tails. Really? And just why is that? I haven't looked into the basis of that claim to have an answer, but I've heard enough people say it and seen enough people pass up pennies that it seems to be widely accepted. Well, not by me!

Here are my thoughts and perspectives on pennies on tails. First, you may or may not have noticed that Abraham Lincoln appears on both sides of a penny. On the tails side, stamped in the center of the Lincoln memorial, you can see a very small figure of Lincoln sitting in a chair. It's a scene from Washington, D.C. So, for those of you concerned that tails is somehow bad luck, Lincoln's head is present on both sides so you have nothing to worry about.

Secondly, no amount of luck should be taken for granted or go unnoticed. I have never counted but probably would have lost count by now if I were keeping track of how many times I heard someone say "it's just a penny". Somehow they are implying that they are above such a low amount of money. Well I have news for you. That penny is money and is in circulation and someone had to work for it and earn it one way or another. For you to just happen to find it for free is incredible and extremely lucky!

If you begin to understand why it is incredible and really just how lucky you are to find it, then you are beginning to understand how luck works. It will test you to see your level of appreciation and acknowledgement. I'm giving you fair advanced notice right now that you are going to see a dramatic increase in your luck and even the amount of pennies you find. I strongly encourage you to go beyond your feelings of hesitation and pride and pick up every one that you see. Keep a separate jar for your "lucky" pennies for a couple months to make it easier to visualize the increase in luck your life is experiencing.

A penny may not seem very significant to you, but what if every person in our country simply gave you one penny of their money? That is essentially what is occurring at a very slow pace. Be very careful not to seem arrogant or too good for any free money. I really wish I could be with you for the next couple weeks to see your reaction when you begin to notice the extra and unexplainable abundance of random pennies that are going to start to occur in your life.

The last change in my thought pattern regarding pennies on the ground has something to do with statistics. Here is the part I mentioned about doubling the amount of money you will find. Statistically, if you flip a coin, there is a 50/50 chance of it landing on one side or the other. No matter how many times you flip a coin, there will always be the same odds. So, theoretically half of the pennies you see are going to be on heads and the other half will be on tails. If you only pick up the pennies that are on heads, you could be missing out on 50% of free money made available to you! Now, enter human superstition into this equation. Let's say most people pass up pennies on tails. Not you though! You now know the potential earnings to be found in the world. Now you have access to 100% of pennies available and half of them out there are going to be left alone just waiting for you to pick them up. You may even see someone walk right past a penny. It's quite possible they won't see it, or think it's just a penny or it could even be on tails. No matter what the reasoning is, you are definitely going to notice an increase in situation such as this.

    I used pennies as a reference, but that definitely is not where a line is drawn. There are so many other ways in which luck is constantly present. We only need to break it down, slow down our lives and notice what is occurring around us. As you hopefully will discover, luck takes on many forms.

PART II

4 RECOGNIZE IT IN EVERY FORM

One of the most important elements when bringing luck and positive energy into your life is to recognize its presence. Luck is something that is easily shrugged off and taken for granted. When first beginning to employ the techniques in this book, you may feel a little silly or absurd. I'm asking you to put any feelings of self-judgment or judgment from others aside.

You must be able to be patient and humble yourself when working with luck and positive energy. Once it begins to flow into your life, it will flow more freely and being humble will also be less of a task and more of a natural action. Luck comes in all shapes and sizes. It isn't always in the form of huge monetary jackpots or winning bets, though it does play a role in those. It might be something as simple as finding a nickel on the ground that later prevented you from having to break a $20 bill.

I use that just as another small example because it occurs frequently with me. It is very important to never write it off as something small no matter how insignificant it may seem to you. If luck is reaching out to you and offering assistance in any way be very accepting and appreciative. I will often use examples comparing luck with children because of the similarity of their nature - Both have the best intentions and no ego and only seek to bring joy to others.

When a child brings you a dandelion or buttercup, they see the beauty of a flower and are giving it as a gift. Without the child in that scenario, many adults would see those as weeds and spend time and money trying to kill and destroy them. I have discovered that luck will test your reaction to determine if it will continue to be abundant in that moment or in future moments. It is very easy to get on a roll with luck and the momentum builds very quickly. Just as quickly as it builds, it can and will evaporate equally as fast if it is not appreciated or treated with respect and kindness. As a matter of fact, it is scared away by negative talk about it or denial. It wants to be known and appreciated.

5 SHOW APPRECIATION

Luck is often involved in all positive experiences in one way shape or form. Granted, hard work pays off and one should never rely fully on luck to bring them though any situation. That would simply be foolish! Think of it as a compliment to your life rather than a foundation. Look back at anything you've worked for and you'll probably discover some variable where luck touched your life. It could be obvious, maybe figuratively microscopic, but usually there is an area where luck played a role.

A very important point to note is that a little appreciation goes a really long way. I make sure to say thanks to luck when it occurs. I just simply speak it out loud right when it happens. Usually I look around and say something like "Wow! That was lucky. Thanks." Or you could call it out by name and simply say "Thanks luck!" I know when I am experiencing a huge rush of luck and it becomes overwhelming, I am amazed and say the word "wow" a lot. When so much luck flows through you and your immediate surroundings, you can't help but be amazed with bewilderment.

No matter how common it may seem in my life, I make sure to always be thankful and appreciative. I'm never arrogant or boastful about my luck either. I share the joy with everyone I know and try to show them an understanding that I am not any more special than they are. Anyone has the potential to be lucky and positive. We are all created equally and can receive the same gifts if we allow them into our life. As with dealing with anything in life, appreciation is very important. Just because you may understand you are just as capable of receiving an abundance of luck and positive energy as anyone else doesn't mean that you are entitled to it.

Remember that luck is a fair and intelligent force of nature. It can be very selective and determines when it wants to come into your life and when it wants to leave. It is there for your convenience and well-being. You can surely make it through life without luck and positive energy. I can assure you that life is a lot easier and more fun when it's filled with luck and positivity. The greatest fact is that it is never too late to make a change in your life or the life of others!

No matter how negative you have been in your life or how unlucky your life may seem, this moment right now can serve as your turning point. You have the free will and decision making power to declare that you want to be lucky and you want to be positive. It simply takes a little commitment to make effort. Once the decision is made and you begin putting forth effort to be positive in your words and actions, more positive energy will flow your way and your luck will increase. In the beginning, you may have to consciously smile on purpose, but you will be working out those muscles. As they become stronger and more defined, your face will become a welcome mat for positive energy and luck will begin to flow your way. I don't want you to simply take my word for it though.

You need to put this into practice to see for yourself and then spread the truth about positive energy and luck to others. Over time, you will see that this is how it works and that by sharing and giving positive words of excitement, you are creating those vibrations in your environment. Before you know it, you will be a source of positive energy people to turn to for inspiration.

Gradually, you will begin to show appreciation for the gifts you will receive. Others will show their appreciation to you for sharing positive energy. Ultimately, you will be showing appreciation to everyone you encounter and clearing the path for luck to flow freely in abundance.

6 LEARN TO RECOGNIZE ITS PRESENCE

When you are first starting to become familiar with luck, it's going to be really subtle. It is so delicate at times that I don't even notice it until I reflect upon my day. It is important that as soon as you experience it, embrace its feeling of presence. When I say to embrace it, just be calm and smile and accept all the feelings that you experience. The more experiences you have with it, the more you will be familiar with it and will have the capability to tune into the vibrations and sensations that alert you of its presence. It could be a sense of mental or visual focus.

If you've ever heard of someone being "in the zone", they were encapsulated by luck and positive energy. I know there are many times that I feel almost like I'm in a trance when my aura is filling up with luck and positive energy. I begin to stare in an unfocused manner in a given direction for no particular reason. I have a gaze that I do not want to break. I can hear all around me and am well aware of my surroundings. It just feels so wonderful to maintain the stare. When those stares happen I make sure to visualize good energy and positive thoughts and focus for as long as I can without trying to force it.

Another very significant feeling I often have when luck is at work is a heat in my chest or stomach. It begins to pulse in my chest and stomach and has its own vibration. Sometimes it gets so intense it feels like it has its own heartbeat. It almost leaves me short of breath. I have checked my pulse during these times and I am as calm as can be and my temperature is normal too. I've also had my health checked too to make sure there isn't an underlying medical condition to be concerned with. Over time, I've made the association that it is a natural part of my life.

Other times you may experience a burst of excitement. Luck can just decide to hit you full force and kick start your energy levels. It isn't always gradual. Think about game show contestants or sports players that make an incredible play or even a normal every-day occurrence when a disaster was averted. There is adrenaline involved and that rush associated with it is also the same type of sensation that luck will bring. Sometimes I have shaking in my hands or speech when I'm in the middle of receiving luck. Usually when it flows heavily, I begin to think it's a little more than my body can handle.

I remember one time specifically when I felt the luck and positive energy welling up from within me. I knew I had to take advantage of it and not let it go to waste. I asked the nearest guy to take note of the time. I said, "Give me two minutes from now!" He asked, "For what?" Rather than wasting time to answer, I simply ran out the door and found the nearest clover patch. Less than two minutes later I returned with fourteen four-leaf clovers. He couldn't believe what he saw and honestly a part of me couldn't believe it either. My hands were shaking very heavily and felt very light and focused. Everything seemed to be glowing and electrified. I managed to capture that moment of luck and positive energy because I had learned to recognize the feelings I was in tune with. (I have a very unexplainable attraction to 4-leaf clovers.)

One way to describe the sensation is that it is similar to extreme nervousness. Anyone who has ever given a speech for the first time or first few times for that matter will understand the feeling.

It is important to note that each person is unique and will have a unique experience. Much like happiness and love and excitement can vary, so can these feelings. I do not know if what I experience is something that you will too. I would love to know what other people experience to discover any common elements.

7 TREAT IT AS A FRIENDLY BEING

I can't stress it enough that luck isn't something that can be seen, but its presence is all around us. Just like wind, oxygen or anything else that can't be seen but we know exists. I can tell you with 100% certainty that luck exists. I'm going to ask you to use your imagination for just a moment. What if trees were all magnets? We wouldn't be able to feel their fields of power as human beings. Anyone could walk around forests freely and unaffected by their properties. The same concept holds true for luck. Its attractive forces and polarity surround us just waiting to have influence over situations and scenarios.

In a sense, our lives are on luck's hidden camera. It is watching us and monitoring our behavior, attitudes and actions. It sees us but we can't see it. How differently would you act if you knew you were being videotaped all the time? Since I know that luck and positive energy is all around, I make sure to be on my best behavior at all times. I'm not claiming to be perfect or the best-behaved human being alive. Rather, I'm aware of my surroundings and put forth my best effort to be as positive as possible.

Knowing that it is around you and that it is wise in its own unique way, consider it a living being and treat it accordingly. If it does grace you with its presence, greet it as you would a guest in your home. It is choosing to be there and didn't just wander into your life. You should feel good about yourself to be chosen by such a powerful and special force. You are doing something right if luck is making the choice to be a part of your life. Take advantage of the opportunity and make a big deal about it. Celebrate the moment with a smile.

It's really important to capture your feelings and define your experience for future reference. The first time you truly experience luck and positive energy you will be overwhelmed. You'll say to yourself that you don't need to write down or record your feelings because it's something you'll never forget. While it is true that it is an unforgettable experience, there are many subtleties that easily slip and dissolve from your memory. It's those little details that you'll want to focus on in the future when trying to recognize and increase your awareness of luck and positive energy when they visit you again.

8 NOT SPOKEN OF

This chapter is a tricky one for me. I have chosen my words very carefully and selectively. Only after reading and understanding this chapter will you comprehend the gaps and contradictions which are present. I do not mean to do a disservice to the reader, but certain elements are required to be omitted. An essential fact when dealing with luck is to treat it as your biggest secret. You have to be very humble in receiving the gifts it offers. I know in other chapters I have said to acknowledge luck's presence and to celebrate it and share with others. Sharing and celebrating doesn't mean being boastful, flagrant or conceited. There are plenty of ways to share your luck and good fortune without revealing your source. In all honesty, when you do something kind for someone or share a positive experience, people generally don't question it too much. Some people may be a little apprehensive, but it's likely they'll be appreciative of your gesture that they won't even care about anything beyond what they are receiving.

Always remember that luck and positive energy are gifts that cost nothing to you. While I mentioned that there is more than enough luck and positive energy for every human alive, it is wise of you to share what is given to you through the gifts you receive. The person or people you share with may not understand and you don't have to explain. You certainly can if you choose. You'll find it more rewarding to share your gifts as a natural part of your day rather than making a big deal about it and drawing attention to yourself. As time moves on and you begin to cultivate more luck and positive energy in your life, you will begin to take on the qualities and properties of luck. The energies will easily flow within you and radiate from your smile that will almost be permanently affixed upon your face.

Never admit directly to having luck but also never outright deny it. This is a very delicate part of the whole experience. The more you allude to or dance around the idea of having luck the better it will be. You can strongly infer or be humble and outspoken about your luck-related experiences. It is best practice to just know it is there. Keep in mind the analogy of the hidden camera always being on. There needs to be a certain mystery always surrounding luck for it to be most potent. Much like a magician never reveals his secrets. He says it's magic, but won't say how. It creates a mystery that somehow something is working that can't be seen or logically explained, but produces a result that is extraordinary. I can't tell you how many times people tell me I'm lucky and I just shrug it off and smirk to myself or pretend I didn't hear them say it.

At this time I would like to mention a phenomenon discovered by scientists, more specifically in the field of Quantum Physics. I know earlier I mentioned that science is always trying to prove nature and forces so as to have a valid explanation and method of predicting what will happen in life as a means to control our environment. Near the end of writing this book, a friend of mine shared knowledge of an experiment with me known as the Double Slit experiment. This experiment was conducted by a man named Thomas Young in 1803. I will give a brief explanation of the overall idea of the experiment, but I encourage you to do a little self-guided research to learn more about this natural phenomenon. It is extremely closely related to the principles and conduct of luck as I have shared with you.

During the experiment, a single slit was created in a vertical wall-like surface. Solid marble-like particles were propelled at the surface to observe the properties of this solid matter. On the other side of the wall was another wall designed to collect the marbles. The result was a pattern in the shape of the slit. This wasn't really much of a surprise. Think of opening a window and squirting a hose right through it. The area on the other side of the window will get most wet where the water was concentrated. Other areas will remain dry. Next, a series of waves were sent toward the same flat wall with a single slit. The space on the other side had a concentration where the slit was.

Next, a wall was introduced with two slits. Again, marbles were used to note the pattern it would form on the other side. As a result, there were two lines on the other side where the slits were. Again, this was not much of a surprise. Next waves were sent to the same surface with two slits and a change was observed. Rather than just two lines formed, there was a series of lines referred to as an interference pattern. There were multiple lines from where different points of waves cancelled each other out and where others made their own point of impact.

For the next stage of the experiment, electrons were introduced to the experiment. While they are microscopic in nature, they are still a solid form of matter and have physical properties just as the marbles do. When they were directed at the wall with a single slit, they formed a single line on the other side, just as the marbles had. These results were consistent with the results from the marbles.

Lastly, the wall with two slits was introduced and something very unique occurred. When the electrons were fired toward the wall with two slits, they formed an interference pattern like the waves had done! This was a baffling occurrence. For some unknown reason, the matter was acting as waves.

So it was determined that closer observations were necessary to study what was taking place. When the electrons were under observation and being studied, they changed their behavior! They started to act like the marbles and no longer formed an interference pattern. Rather, they formed two lines on the other side as was originally expected and anticipated.

Much like luck does not like to be predicted, controlled or manipulated, neither did the electrons in this experiment. There is a clear similarity between Young's experiment and my life-long observations of the patterns and behaviors of luck and positive energy.

9 NEVER TAKE IT FOR GRANTED

There is going to come a time when luck is going to flow toward you more than you realized was ever possible. It is going to become so commonplace that you may have the tendency to become complacent about it. I like to think about celebrities or anyone famous I know about but who have never met that I admire. There are many people that have more money and fame than they know what to do with, yet they still maintain a humble and generous spirit. I suggest that you adopt that frame of mind and attitude and make it become genuine if you want the luck and positive energy to continue to flow within your life. In a sense, luck feeds on itself.

I have definitely noticed that the more it is acknowledged and appreciated, the more present and comfortable it becomes when interacting with your life. It is imperative that you never take it for granted. You must respond to each experience as being as unexplainable and mystifying as the first occurrence. When you start to take it for granted or expecting it to occur, that's when you may begin to form the attitude that you are somehow in control or entitled to have luck.

Think back to previous chapters when I mentioned showing appreciation for it. It will leave you if you act ungrateful, unappreciative or as if you have control of it. One of the great facts about luck, however, is that it can return just as quickly as it left. It will not hold a grudge or act as a human does based on past performance. There are simply conditions that must be present in order for luck to exist.

The most basic example that comes to mind is when growing a plant. Three main things must be present- soil, water, and sunlight. With those basic elements, a plant will survive. Of course, there are many ways in which you can improve and maximize conditions to help the plant achieve its fullest potential existence. The same holds true for luck. Most people experience luck in their lives from time to time. Being aware of the conditions required by luck and utilizing the skills and techniques I have shared with you will produce a higher yield and an abundance of its fruits.

CONCLUSION

This book shares a lot of insight into a world that surrounds us that so many are blind to or unable to define. I ask you again to please have an open mind and an open heart when reflecting upon the information contained here within. Also, please understand the great knowledge and responsibility that lies in your hands. I'm pretty certain that some people are going to understand what I've stated, some are going to be unsure of the reality of what I've stated, some are going to be slightly skeptical and willing to try some of the ideas I have shared and some are going to be outright against everything I have said.

One thing I ask you to do now that you have completed this book is to view it as a guide to living with other human beings. Everything I've shared has personified luck as a living entity. If nothing else, use this book as a guide to live your life among the people who you encounter. If you follow the rules and guidelines I have laid out for you, there will be an improvement in your personal relationships. Be humble in your relationships. Don't take them for granted. Any kind gesture made to you should not go unnoticed. Show appreciation and recognition for everything done in your favor. Never let fear of judgment from others or yourself dictate your behavior and kindness toward someone else. I wish you great luck for the rest of your life and hope that I have been able to make your world a better place.

ABOUT THE AUTHOR

Tony Wargo was born and raised in Hampton Roads, Virginia. He has a wife, Jennifer and a daughter, Olivia. He earned his Bachelor's degree in Business Administration from ECPI University. He has been playing drums since 1992 and appreciates everything about nature.

He loves spending quality time with his family. During the warmer months, he enjoys spending his time in the Outer Banks of North Carolina. He is often in the Atlantic Ocean on his boogie board or just relaxing on the beach. He also enjoys collecting 4-Leaf clovers any time he spots a patch. He has his own business selling 4-Leaf clovers with a wide variety of options.

Tony would love to hear stories from his readers! Share your stories and testimonials about how reading this book has increased luck and positive energy in your life.

Visit the website for more details!
www.artofwargo.com

www.ingramcontent.com/pod-product-compliance
Lightning Source LLC
Chambersburg PA
CBHW071414040426
42444CB00009B/2250